1

MW01288611

ENGLAND

Travel Guide Book

A Comprehensive 5-Day Travel Guide to London,
England
& Unforgettable English Travel

♦ *Travel Guides to Europe Series* ♦

Passport to European Travel Guides

❧

Eye on Life Publications

London, England Travel Guide Book
Copyright © 2015 Passport to European Travel Guides

ISBN 10: 1517448603
ISBN 13: 978-1517448608

~

Other Travel Guide Books by Passport to European Travel Guides

Paris, France

Provence & the French Riviera, France

Santorini, Greece

Barcelona, Spain

Istanbul, Turkey

Vienna, Austria

Budapest, Hungary

Prague, Czech Republic

Rome, Italy

Venice, Italy

Florence, Italy

Naples & the Amalfi Coast, Italy

Top 10 Travel Guide to Italy

Top 10 Travel Guide to France

"By seeing London, I have seen as much of life as the world can show." —Samuel Johnson

Table of Contents

• Map of London, England •

• Introduction •

London, England.

On center stage in Europe, London is a richly diverse and cultured city with some of the world's most well known sights: **Buckingham Palace, Big Ben, Westminster Abbey,** the **Houses of Parliament,** the **London Eye, Tower Bridge,** the **Tower of London,** the **Tate Modern** and more. London is also home to some of the world's best theater, exciting nightlife, great shopping, cool pubs, and captivating history. And, of course, what's England without their royals? All its facets unite to make the city of London, England one of the most visited tourist destinations in the world.

In this 5-day guide to London, you'll find a variety of our top recommendations and helpful tips to prepare you for having the best travel experience in England! **Read over the insider tips** carefully and familiarize yourself with the information on preparing for your trip. **Every traveler** has different preferences, and we've included a wide range of recommendations to suit all tastes and budgets.

You're welcome to follow our detailed **5-day itinerary** to the letter, or you can **mix and match** the activities at your own discretion.

Most importantly, we know you're sure to have a great time and enjoy the wonderful city that is London, England!

Enjoy!

The Passport to European Travel Guides Team

• City Snapshot •

Language: English

Local Airports: Heathrow, Gatwick, Luton, Stansted, and London City.

Currency: Great British Pound Sterling (£ / GBP).

Country Code: 44

Emergencies: Dial 112 or 999

• Before You Go... •

✓ Have a Passport

If you don't already have one, you'll need to apply for a passport in your home country a good two months before you intend to travel, to avoid cutting it too close. You'll need to find a local passport agency, complete an application, take fresh photos of yourself, have at least one form of ID and pay an application fee. If you're in a hurry, you can usually expedite the application for a 2-3 week turnaround at an additional cost.

✓ Need a Visa?

To find out if you need a visa to enter England and how to apply for it, see the **GOV.UK website** or check with your local British embassy or local consulate before you travel. The rules change regularly, so it's best to check well in advance of your planned trip. https://www.gov.uk/standard-visitor-visa

✓ Healthcare

Prior to your trip, you should **purchase a travel insurance** to cover any medical expenses in case you should become ill or have an accident while in the UK. If you have general health insurance, you should first check with them to see what coverage you have (if any) when traveling abroad. This is always the best way to go, since whether or not you have your own insurance can greatly impact the type of care you receive, the when, where and how.

For residents of the United Kingdom, England has a nationalized public health service, the **National Health Service (NHS).** However, visitors are not eligible for free medical services, except in the case of an emergency while in the UK.

If you happen to come from a country that has a healthcare agreement with the UK, you can receive free medical treatment if you need it immediately for a condition that started subsequent to your arrival in the UK.

Visitors from within Europe need to carry a valid EHIC (European Health Insurance Card) and present it at the time of treatment.

✓ Set the Date

Since temperatures can dip quite low in the **wintertime**, we think **spring** is the ideal time to visit London. Temps are milder and everything is in bloom! **Fall** is also a good time, though usually a bit nippier.

✓ Pack

• We recommend **packing only the essentials** needed for the season in which you'll be traveling. By far, the most important thing to pack is a good pair of **walking** shoes (water-resistant if you're traveling in colder months, and comfortable, light sandals or sneakers to walk good distances in warmer months).

• **A backpack** can be handy during the day when you go out sightseeing and collecting souvenirs, particularly when getting on and off buses, boats, trains or trams.

• If you're planning on visiting the beautiful **cathedrals of London**, be sure to pack **clothes that appropriately cover** your shoulders and legs. **In the colder months,** bring a warm sweater, clothes you can layer, and a rain jacket or umbrella. And even though, London is famous for overcast skies, always pack **sunscreen, sunglasses, and a hat.**

• **Hand sanitizer** is always great to have along with you when traveling.

• **Medication.** Don't forget to have enough for the duration of your trip. It's also helpful to have a **note from your physician** in case you're questioned for carrying a certain quantity.

• A simple **first aid kit** is always a good idea to have in your luggage, just in case.

• You can bring one or two **reusable shopping bags** for bringing souvenirs home.

• **Travelers from outside Europe** will need to bring along a **universal electrical plug converter** that can work for both lower and higher voltages. This way you'll be able to plug in your cell phones, tablets, curling irons, etc., during the trip.

• Be sure to **leave expensive jewels and high-priced electronics at home.** Like most major cities and tourist attractions, thieves and pickpockets abound. Avoid making yourself a target.

• **Take pictures of your travel documents and your passport** and email them to yourself before your trip. This can help in the unfortunate event they are lost or stolen.

• **Pack well,** but be sure to leave room for souvenirs!

✓ Phone Home

How will you call home from England? Does your cell phone company offer service while abroad? **What are their rates?**

There are many ways to **call home** from Europe that are inexpensive or completely free.

You may also **sign up for roaming or Internet hotspot** through your own cell phone provider. You can also use Skype, WhatsApp, Viper, or many other voice-over IP providers that are entirely free.

You can also buy an inexpensive, **pre-paid local phone** or **phone chip** for your phone — which also gives you a local phone number. **Calling cards** are used less and less these days, but they're also an option.

✓ Currency Exchange

England uses the **pound sterling** (£) as its currency. Check the current **currency exchange rates** prior to your trip, as they change daily. You can do it online using this or many other online currency exchange calculators, or through your bank:
http://www.xe.com/currencyconverter

✓ Contact Your Embassy

In the unfortunate event that you should lose your passport or be victimized while away, **your country's embassy** will be able to help you. Be sure to give your itinerary and contact information to a close **friend or family member**, then also contact your embassy with your emergency contact information before you leave.

✓ Your Mail

Ask a neighbor to **check your mailbox** while you're away or visit your local post office and request a hold. **Overflowing mailboxes** are a dead giveaway that no one's home.

• Getting in the Mood •

Here are a few great books and films set in or about London that we recommend you watch in preparation for your trip to this much-esteemed locale!

What to Read:

One of the great books to read before your trip to London is <u>*Love, Nina*</u> by Nina Stibbe. In the early 80s, the 20-year-old Nina moves to London to work as a nanny for two young boys, the sons of editor Mary-Kay Wilmers and her ex-husband, director Stephan Frears. Nina shares experiences in many letters to her sister. The book is lots of fun, hilarious, charming, and touching.

Another great novel to read before your trip is <u>*White Teeth*</u> by Zadie Smith. This book focuses on two wartime friends and their families in a suburb of London. The novel features a richly diverse cast of cultures, including Jewish, Afro-Caribbean and Muslim. Great reading!

And our final book recommendation, <u>*London Fields*</u> by Martin Amis, is perfect preparation for your trip! It's part murder mystery, part dark comedy, based in London. An American writer living in London has had writer's block for 20 years when he becomes seriously ill. The supporting characters—Keith, the cheat, and Nicola, the murderee—round out this engaging story.

What to Watch:

One of the greatest romantic comedies of recent times is, of course, _Love Actually,_ directed by Richard Curtis. It's a must-watch before your trip to London, even if you've seen it before! Set primarily in London, this heart-warming story full of twists and turns begins a few weeks before Christmas and unfolds in a countdown to the holiday. It definitely puts you in the right mood for a trip to London!

Another great flick with a London backdrop is _**Notting Hill**_, starring Julia Roberts and Hugh Grant. Will (Hugh Grant) owns an indie bookshop in the Notting Hill district of London. He is divorced and now has an eccentric flat mate named Spike. Will meets Hollywood megastar Anna Scott (Julia Roberts) when she visits the bookshop, and a complicated relationship unfolds from there.

On another note, _**Dirty Pretty Things**_ with Audrey Tautou is a harrowing dramatic thriller about struggle and survival for two immigrants when they discover just how much is for sale in London's secret underworld. Gripping!

• Local Tourist Information •

As soon as you arrive at the airport, you can pick up **brochures, city maps**, and other helpful information from the regional tourism board. You can also ask any question you may have about accommodations or things to during your stay.

Also, most hotels and B&B's in London will have **maps** available for their guests, as well as **tips** about local restaurants, museums, and seasonal events.

• About the Airports •

London is one of the most well connected cities in the world, with five international airports and a high-speed Eurostar railway. It is also quite central, as more than 50 countries are just a three-hour flight from London.

The airports within London's vicinity: Heathrow, Gatwick, Luton, Stansted, and London City.

Heathrow is in the London Borough of Hillingdon. The largest of London's airports, it's considered the international gateway of the United Kingdom.

Visit the airport websites:

Heathrow Airport:
http://www.heathrowairport.com
Gatwick Airport: http://www.gatwickairport.com
Stansted Airport: http://www.stanstedairport.com
Luton Airport: http://www.london-luton.co.uk/en
London City Airport:
http://www.londoncityairport.com

• How Long is the Flight? •

- The flight from **Paris to London** is approx. 1 hour

- From **NYC to London** is approx. 7 hours

- From **Miami to London** is approx. 8.5 hours

- From **Los Angeles to London** is approx. 10.5 hours

- From **Moscow to London** is approx. 4 hours

- From **Hong Kong to London** is approx. 13 hours

- From **Cape Town to London** is approx. 12 hours

- From **Sydney to London** is approx. 22.5 hours

• Overview of London, England •

The history of London dates back thousands of years, and the city is currently home to four World Heritage Sites: **Westminster Abbey**, the **Palace of Westminster**, the **Tower of London**, the **Royal Botanic Gardens, Kew,** and **Maritime Greenwich**.

Many of the city's attractions are free to the public, such as the famous art galleries, **National Gallery** and **Tate Modern**.

Divided into 33 boroughs (districts, 12 comprise "**Inner London**" and the other 20 make up "**Outer London**"), London is also considered Europe's best **destination for shopping**, and boasts many well-visited **pubs and restaurants** serving up international flare and flavor. **Diversity** and **cultural blends** thrive throughout the city and there's so much to discover and enjoy!

• Insider Tips For Tourists •

Etiquette

• **"British" Etiquette:** Residents of England are considered and can be called "British." And when referring to the person's heritage, you can say they are "English."

• **Meet & Greet Etiquette:** Brits admire people who are **quiet**, restrained, **very polite**, and non-abrasive. When meeting someone, a light handshake is sufficient, unless you know the person very well. In general, the English **do not touch** or **display affection in public**.

• **Restaurant Etiquette:** Gently raise your hand to call the waiter. It's considered impolite to wave or call out.

• **Sightseeing Etiquette:** Jaywalking is common in England. On escalators, especially on the tube, the right side is for standing, and the left is for those who prefer to walk along.

• **It's impolite** not to say **'please'** and **'thank you'** when seeking and/or offered assistance in any capacity.

• **Avoid speaking loudly** when in public, especially when using your **cell phone**. It's considered poor manners.

• **Never cut in line** (called a 'queue' in England). This can get you nasty looks, or even thrown out of an establishment altogether.

Time Zone

London and the country of England are in the GMT time zone (Greenwich Mean Time). There's a **5-hour time difference** between **New York and London**. London is ahead on the clock. When it's 8AM in New York, it's 1PM in London.

The format for abbreviating dates in Europe is different from the US. They use: day/month/year, so 6/9/20 means September 6, 2020 to Europeans.

Saving Time & Money

• If you're looking to save money, avoid taking too many cabs, as the fares are pricey. An **Oyster card** can save you lots on getting around in London. It's rechargeable and probably the least expensive way to travel about town, with access to buses, the tube system, etc., all in one). Children under the age of ten can travel for free with the purchase of an adult ticket: https://account.tfl.gov.uk/oyster

• We recommend finding a family run B&B for your **accommodations**. There are many affordable options in the King's Cross area and west of the British Museum.

• London also has some great hostels if you're comfortable with that type of accommodation. See our upcoming recommendations on **budget sleeps!**

For more privacy, you can consider **renting a London apartment**. This gives you the comfort of a home with a **fully equipped kitchen**. You can cook your meals and save on the **cost of dining out** for every meal, which certainly adds up.

• Many of London's museums have **free admission** (the British Museum, V&A, Tate Modern, National Gallery, etc.).

• For great **bargain shopping**, go to Notting Hill and stroll along Portobello Road. There are many treasures to be found in this famous neighborhood — go and explore! Also, other neighborhood markets offer great deals and assortments of products.

• **Many popular restaurants** and shops have their menus and pricing on their websites. It's a good idea to check out prices and **plan ahead** if you're on a budget. It's always a good idea to **book as many things as possible** (museum passes, attraction tickets, etc.) **in advance.**

Tipping

• **It's customary** to leave **10-15% of the bill** when you dine out. UK restaurants often add on a service charge (usually 12.5%), especially for large parties, so **check your bill** before tipping.

• **It's not customary** to tip for fast food, self-service, in pubs or bars, or for takeout food (called 'takeaway' in England).

• **In hotels,** you should tip the bellman who helps you with your bags £1 pound per bag is good. You may also tip the chambermaid a couple pounds for stays longer than 1-2 nights. You don't have to tip room service.

• **In a bar or pub**, you don't have to top the bartender. Locals who develop a rapport may buy him a drink or tip about £1.

• If you get a **spa treatment**, tipping is not expected.

• **In hair salons**, tip about 10% if you're happy.

When You Have to Go

Going to the bathroom is very easy in London. There are many public restrooms available all over the place. Just ask.

Taxes

Value Added Tax (VAT) a consumption sales tax throughout Europe. As of this writing, the standard rate in England is 20%. Reduced VAT rates apply for pharmaceuticals, passenger transport, admission to cultural and entertainment events, hotels, restaurants and on foodstuffs, medical and books.

Visitors from outside the UK may be eligible for a **VAT refund** if certain criteria are met: 1) you do not live in the UK 2) you must be leaving the UK within 3 months of the purchase 3) purchase must be made in a shop or business that participates in the Retail Export Scheme or Tax Free Shopping program 4) purchases must meet the minimum of typically £75.

To obtain a VAT refund, ask the shop attendant for the **VAT 407** form (participating shops usually have some sort of signage, but if not, just ask). You will need to present the form to customs at the airport for processing.

Phone Calls

The **country code** for England is 44.

When calling home from London, first dial 00. You will then hear a tone. Then dial the country code (1 for the U.S. and Canada, 44 for the UK, 61 for Australia, 7 for Russia, 81 for Japan, and 86 for China), then the area code without any initial 0, then the actual phone number.

Electricity

Electricity in England, as in the rest of Europe, is at an average of **230 volts** alternating at about 50 cycles per second (to compare, the U.S. averages 110 volts, alternating at about 60 cycles per second.) As discussed before, when traveling from outside of Europe, you will need to **bring an adapter and converter** that enable you to plug your electronics and appliances into **the sockets** they use.

Cell phone, tablet and laptop chargers are typically dual voltage, so you won't need a converter, just an adapter to be able to plug them in. Most small appliances are likely to be dual voltage, but **always double**

check when possible, especially to avoid frying hair dryers and travel irons.

In Emergencies

Dial 112 for all emergencies in the European Union: police, ambulance and fire. Calls are answered in English, Italian, French, and German. In London, you can also **dial 999** for emergency help.

Holidays

England has a number of bank, public and traditional holidays and national events throughout the year. Here is a list of the main public holidays:

January 1 — New Year's Day

March 17 — St. Patrick's Day

Friday before Easter — Good Friday

Easter — 1st Sunday after the first full moon on or after the March equinox

December 25 — Christmas Day

December 26 — Boxing Day

Hours of Operation

The London tube system doesn't run 24 hours a day. Typically, it starts running at 5:00 am and stops after midnight.

Most stores are open from 9:00 am until 5:30 or 6:00 pm, Monday through Saturday. Some grocery stores close late, around 10:00 pm, but it's best to double-check, depending on the area.

Banks are usually open Monday through Friday, 9:30 am until 2:30 pm, and 9:30 am until noon on Saturdays. They are closed on Sundays. Some banks offer later hours and close at 5:00 pm.

Businesses are typically open Monday through Friday from 9:00 am until 5:30 pm and **government offices** 9:30 am until 4:30 pm.

Money

As we mentioned, the UK's currency is the **pound sterling** (£ / GBP). Despite being a member of the European Union, the UK does not use the euro.

It's best not to carry more than **£150 in cash** at any given time. In the event of loss or theft, this will minimize your damages.

It's best to utilize **ATMs** and tellers in the **non-tourist areas** of the city and be sure to use common sense and not make yourself a target for pickpockets. If anyone approaches you unexpectedly, it's best to politely keep walking.

Also, **beware the unnecessary fees.** If you're given the option to pay in dollars vs. pounds when using your credit card, simply say no. Paying in dollars **will cost you more** in fees and you may or may not be informed of the additional charges at the time of the transaction.

• Climate and Best Times to Travel •

London is known for pretty finicky, overcast, rainy weather. **August** is usually the warmest time of the year, when the temperature can hit 90°F, but generally averages about 70°F.

London is also a year-round destination, so the major tourist attractions are not seasonal, although it is **most crowded** in the **summer months** (July and August).

As previously mentioned, we think **spring** or **fall** is the best times of year to visit London.

Transportation

London's Underground rail network ("the Tube") is typically the quickest and easiest way to get around. It's super easy to navigate, inexpensive, and you can plan your trip using the tools offered on the Tube's official website:
https://www.tfl.gov.uk/modes/tube

London buses are a quick, convenient and inexpensive way to travel around the city, with plenty of sightseeing opportunities on all routes. **Docklands Light Railway** (DLR) is driverless and serves areas of East and South East London, including Canary Wharf.

For a more leisurely commute, London also has a **river bus service** operated by **MBNA Thames Clippers**. Riverboats depart from various River Thames ports every 20 minutes and run through the heart of London, offering great sightseeing views along the way. It's one of our favorite ways to see London!
http://www.thamesclippers.com

Driving

To the left, to the left. Remember they **drive on the left side** of the road in the UK.

We don't recommend driving in London for first-time visitors from outside the UK, especially in central London during rush hour. As we've said, the city has an excellent public transportation system for getting from point A to point B.

However, if you should be inclined to **rent a car** for day trips outside the city, etc., be sure to **get a GPS** and **learn the basic rules** of the road. **Seatbelts** are required, **car seats** for children and **helmets** for motorcyclists. For **the complete driving requirements**, see the government's **Department For Transport's website**:
https://www.gov.uk/government/organisations/department-for-transport

• Tours •

London By Bike

London is a large city and trying to cover *everything* on foot can be a bit of a challenge for anyone. Take advantage of some of the awesome bike tours available and cover some of your itinerary on wheels!

We think **Fat Tire Bike Tours** is one of the best in London. Their **"Royal London"** and **"River Thames"** bike tours are the most popular and offer great insights into the history of London and England as a whole.

Fat Tire Bike Tour of London
Tel: +44 7882 338 779
http://london.fattirebiketours.com

Tally Ho! Cycle Tours is another cycling company that offers fun, expansive tours of London. We recommend the "**London Landmarks**" and "**Gin & Food**" tours!

Tally Ho! Cycle Tours
Address: 213 Carlisle Lane, London SE1 7LH, United Kingdom
Tel: +44 7969 230828 or +44 203 4880297
http://www.tallyhocycletours.com

London By Boat

City Cruises offers cool river cruises and Thames boat tours from Westminster, Tower and Greenwich Piers. Depending on your preference, you can take a traditional cruise around the city, a dinner cruise, or choose the Elvis Rock the Boat cruise!

City Cruises
Address: Lower Thames Street, London
Tel: +44 20 77 400 400
http://www.citycruises.com

Another interesting option is a boat tour called **Tate to Tate.** This tour runs every 40 minutes and connects the two Tate galleries: Tate Modern and Tate Britain. It takes you right through the heart of London.

Tate to Tate
Address: Bankside, London, SE1 9TG
http://www.tateatate.org

London By Bus

The Original London Sightseeing Tour company offers hop-on, hop-off sightseeing tours of London by open-top, red double-decker bus. We like it a lot and think you should definitely experience London this way, particularly for kids and elderly travelers. Tickets include free admission to London walking tours and free admission to the Thames River cruise.

The Original London Sightseeing Tour
Address: Jews Row, Wandsworth, London SW18 1TB, United Kingdom
Tel: +44 20 8877 1722
http://www.theoriginaltour.com

Big Bus London also has good deals on tours of all of the major attractions in London, in 12 different languages and it also comes with free admission to the Thames River cruise or guided walking tours of London. It's a great deal! You truly get to experience the city from a variety of perspectives.

Big Bus London
Tel: +44 20 7808 6753
http://eng.bigbustours.com/london/home.html

Try Special Interest or Walking Tours

Tour the Commons and Lords Chambers and the historic Westminster Hall with **Tours of Parliament**. Specialty tours are also available if you happen to be interested to get more in-depth information about the British Parliament system. We suggest researching the options before booking.

Tours of the Parliament
Address: Westminster, London SW1A 0AA, United Kingdom
Tel: +44 20 7219 3000
http://www.parliament.uk/visiting/visiting-and-tours/tours-of-parliament

How about seeing London by Helicopter? British Tours offers an amazing half-day helicopter tour of all of the city's popular sites!

British Tours
Address: 615 Linen Hall, 162-168 Regent Street, London W1B 5TE, United Kingdom
Tel: + 44 20 7038 0688
http://www.britishtours.com/london-helicopter-tours

The London Bridge Experience and Tombs is a great tour to book online if you enjoy being spooked and like the macabre!

The London Bridge Experience and Tombs
https://www.thelondonbridgeexperience.com

And if you really enjoy the macabre, another great option is the London Walk's **Jack the Ripper Walking Tour**, which leaves for a grisly trek through the city at 7:30 pm each night.

Jack the Ripper Walking Tour
Tel: +44 20 7624 3978
http://www.jacktheripperwalk.com

Interested in seeing how and where the locals live? Try the **Residential London** tour by British Tours. You get to pick the areas, from the ultra chic town of Mayfair to the fashionable Chelsea district.

British Tours
Address: 615 Linen Hall, 162-168 Regent Street, London W1B 5TE, United Kingdom
Tel: + 44 20 7038 0688
http://www.britishtours.com/residential-london-tour

• 5 Days In London! •

There is so much to see and do in and around London that it will be hard for you to do it all in just 5 days! **Enjoy this 5-day itinerary** for a well balanced, easy-going, fun and memorable experience! Modify or adjust if you like! Also, be sure to **check websites or call ahead** for the most recent hours and pricing information.

• Day 1 •

Once you arrive at your hotel (or wherever you're staying) relax a bit, get settled and then freshen up before venturing out to explore the surrounding area. (It's best to arrive in the morning.)

You can also head over to the world-renowned **British Museum.** Founded in 1753, the Museum's collection spans over two million years of human history! You get to see the works of the biggest names in European art history on display here and **admission is free**.

Another option is **The National Gallery**. Thousands of European paintings and drawings from the Middle Ages to the 20th century are displayed here, from Leonardo da Vinci and Rembrandt, to Renoir and Van Gogh. They also have special exhibitions, insightful lectures, special programs, guided tours, and holiday events for kids and adults available.

Lunch at Tas restaurant. It's near the British Museum and serves up delicious Turkish fare! If you've never eaten Turkish, today's a great day to give it a go! It's best to call ahead for reservations.

After lunch, how about going to see the world famous **Tate Modern?** A visit to London wouldn't be complete without a trip to this hot spot. If you're not up for it today, definitely fit it in by the end of your trip! Tate Modern is Britain's national museum of modern and contemporary art from around the globe. Admission is free.

Next, you must get yourself over to **Covent Garden**, a famous London district rich with great shopping, food and drink. In this case, focus on the food and devour **the best fish and chips in London** from the **Rock & Sole Plaice!** It's finger licking good (but please don't do too much of that in London), and once you've had fish and chips here, you'll be spoiled for having it anywhere else!

Alternatively, a stroll through **Trafalgar Square** might be in order if your not looking for the best fish and chips. It's the largest square in London; a public space and major tourist attraction in the City of Westminster that features cool statues and good people watching. This square is also used for political rallies and community assemblies, such as the yearly New Year's Eve celebration. Take a nice stroll through on your first day in London, but be sure to look out for the pigeons!

For dinner tonight, we recommend Gordon Ramsay's **Maze Grill** in the heart of southwest London. They serve up American fare of steak, fish and chicken that tastes great!

Location Information

British Museum
Address: Great Russell Street, London WC1B 3DG, United Kingdom
Tel: +44 20 7323 8299
http://www.britishmuseum.org

The National Gallery
Address: Trafalgar Square, London WC2N 5DN, United Kingdom
Tel: +44 20 7747 2885
http://www.nationalgallery.org.uk

Tas (Bloomsbury)
Address: 22 Bloomsbury Street, London, City of London, Greater London WC1B 3QJ, United Kingdom
Tel: +44 20 7637 4555
http://www.tasrestaurants.co.uk/bloomsbury.html

Tate Modern
Address: Bankside, London SE1 9TG, United Kingdom
Tel: +44 20 7887 8888
http://www.tate.org.uk

Covent Garden (West End)
http://www.coventgardenlondonuk.com

Rock & Sole Plaice (Covent Garden)
Address: 9aj, 47 Endell Street, London WC2H 9AJ, United Kingdom
Tel: +44 20 7836 3785
http://www.rockandsoleplaice.com

Trafalgar Square
Address: Trafalgar Square, Westminster, London WC2N 5DN, United Kingdom
Tel: +44 20 7983 4750

Maze Grill
Address: 79 Royal Hospital Road, London SW3 4HP, United Kingdom
Tel: +44 20 7352 4448
http://www.gordonramsay.com/royalhospitalroad

• Day 2 •

After a nice breakfast at your hotel, head over to the **Victoria and Albert Museum** (V&A), one of the world's greatest museums for art and design, houses an enduring collection of over 4.5 million pieces and exhibits that span from ancient times to modern day! **Admission is free.**

In recent years, the V&A has undergone quite the restoration as well. Highlights include the Medieval Renaissance galleries, which contain some of the greatest surviving treasures from the period, the spectacular Jeweler Gallery, and lots more. Less well known is its **Museum of Childhood** in Bethnal Green, where a vast collection of childhood-related objects, some dating back decades (and, in some cases, even centuries) are displayed.

Next up, a visit to Her Majesty's Royal Palace and Fortress, a.k.a. the **Tower of London.** Despite its dark reputation as being a place of torture and demise, there's great history to be discovered here. Watch for the famous Tower of London ravens that gather here frequently.

For lunch, head over to the nearby **St. Katharine Docks** and have a great pizza at **The Dickens Inn Pizzeria.** We love the atmosphere and they serve delicious pizzas, salads and pastas.

After lunch, stroll leisurely along the docks and enjoy the shops before making your way over to **Piccadilly Circus** (about 12 minutes away on the Tube) for more great shopping and entertainment in the West End. This area is especially known for the neon signs and video displays, so it's also a great spot to visit at nighttime.

For dinner we recommend **Goddards at Greenwich.** Stop in and have a great plate of pie and mash, traditional London fare!

In the evening after dinner, take a walk over to the Parliament Building at the **Palace of Westminster**. It's a dynamite view at night and, of course, **Big Ben** is a must-see in London. "Big Ben" is the nickname for the Great Bell of the clock at the Palace of Westminster's northern end. You can also come back here during the day for a **Parliament tour**.

Location Information

Victoria and Albert Museum
Address: Cromwell Road, London SW7 2RL, United Kingdom
Tel: +44 20 7942 2000
http://www.vam.ac.uk

V&A Museum of Childhood
Address: Cambridge Heath Road, London E2 9PA, United Kingdom
Tel: +44 20 8983 5200
http://www.vam.ac.uk/moc

Tower of London
Address: London EC3N 4AB, United Kingdom
Tel: +44 844 482 7777
http://www.hrp.org.uk/TowerOfLondon

The Dickens Inn (Pizzeria on 2nd floor)
Address: Marble Quay, St Katharine Docks, Saint Katharine's Way, London E1W 1UH, United Kingdom
Tel: +44 20 7488 2208
http://www.dickensinn.co.uk/pizza

Goddards at Greenwich
Address: 22 King William Walk, London SE10 9HU, United Kingdom
Tel: +44 20 8305 9612
http://www.goddardsatgreenwich.co.uk

Palace of Westminster
Address: Westminster, London SW1A 0AA, United Kingdom
Tel: +44 20 7219 3000
http://www.parliament.uk/visiting/visiting-and-tours/tours-of-parliament

• Day 3 •

After breakfast this morning, you can head over to the world famous **Madame Tussauds,** a museum chain with a location in central London full of wax statues of celebrities and well known public figures. Go check out your favorite famous faces!

And of course, a trip to London cannot be complete without a visit to the **Buckingham Palace,** the London residence of the British royal family and the monarchy's administrative headquarters.

If you're in London in August or September, be sure to get tickets to tour the staterooms used for official and state entertaining. They're only open to the public each year in August and September.

If you time your visit well, you can get to see the changing of the guards at the palace. You may also get to see the guards riding on horseback in their big hats.

Next, have lunch at the wonderful **Café Bella Maria**, just a short walk from Buckingham Palace. It's a gem of a place to have a nice British or Italian bite to eat before making your way to the **London Dungeon,** a cool tourist attraction that recreates various scary historical events geared toward younger audiences. They use a blend of live actors, special effects, and scary rides and it's loads of fun! Though not for the faint of heart, older kids, teenagers, and many adults, love it. Book your tickets in advance.

Next we have a treat for literary and murder mystery buffs: **The Sherlock Holmes Museum**. The fictional Sherlock Holmes and Dr. Watson lived at 221b Baker Street, right? Well, that's the location of the real-life Sherlock Holmes Museum! Go check out the wonderful exhibits and interiors that have been lovingly dedicated to these iconic characters.

Take a stroll through the beautiful and royal **Hyde Park** at the end of your day and relax a bit. Alternatively, there are many activities you can get into here: swimming, tennis, horseback riding, boating or biking. Be sure to visit the famous Speakers' Corner, located in the center of the park. Lots of open public  debate and discussion take place there. Perhaps you'll be inspired to speak?

Hyde Park is also neighbor to **Kensington Gardens**, another great royal park site to see.

It's been a long day, so you may just want to head back to your hotel and grab dinner there or someplace nearby. Tomorrow awaits!

Location Information

Madame Tussauds
Address: Marylebone Road, London NW1 5LR, United Kingdom
Tel: +44 871 894 3000
https://www.madametussauds.com/London

Buckingham Palace
Address: London SW1A 1AA, United Kingdom
Tel: +44 20 7766 7300
http://www.royal.gov.uk/theroyalresidences/buckinghampalace/buckinghampalace.aspx

Café Bella Maria
Address: 4 Lower Grosvenor Place | Victoria, London SW1W 0EJ, England
Tel: +44 20 7976 6280
http://www.cafebellamaria.co.uk

London Dungeon
Address: Riverside Building, County Hall, Westminster Bridge Rd, City of London, Greater London SE1 7PB, United Kingdom
Tel: +44 871 423 2240
http://www.thedungeons.com/london/en

The Sherlock Holmes Museum
Address: 221b Baker Street, London NW1 6XE, United Kingdom
Tel: +44 20 7224 3688
http://www.sherlock-holmes.co.uk

Hyde Park
Address: London, United Kingdom
Tel: +44 300 061 2000
https://www.royalparks.org.uk/parks/hyde-park

Kensington Gardens
Address: London W2 2UH, United Kingdom
Tel: +44 300 061 2000
https://www.royalparks.org.uk/parks/kensington-gardens

• Day 4 •

There are many options for **day trips** outside of London. The one we like best is to **Windsor Castle, Stonehenge & Bath**. A fabulously historic site, Windsor Castle was built on a lush hill overlooking the River Thames. The Castle houses priceless works of art by Rembrandt and Leonardo da Vinci. You may also visit **St. George's Chapel** and **Queen Mary's Dolls' House** at Windsor. Plan to spend at least a half-day (12 hours) for the trip to Windsor Castle.

Stonehenge is a prehistoric monument in Wiltshire, England. One of the most famous sites in the world, Stonehenge is the remains of a ring of standing stones set within earthworks of the Neolithic Age.

Trip Advisor's Viator offers a great **day trip package** for Windsor Castle, Stonehenge & Bath:

http://www.viator.com/tours/London/Stonehenge -Windsor-Castle-and-Bath-Day-Trip-from- London/d737-3858EE021

Alternative itinerary for a great day trip out of London:

Are you a fan of Downton Abbey? Well, today you should definitely take a day trip to **Highclere Castle** where the show was filmed! **This trip** will last about half a day as well, so plan to be gone at least 10 hours. Enjoy!

http://www.londontoolkit.com/tours/premium_do wnton_abbey.htm

When you get back to London, if you haven't had **dinner**, we suggest the **Meraz Café**, a casual Indian café that serves really good food.

Location Information

Windsor Castle
Address: Windsor, Windsor and Maidenhead SL4 1NJ, United Kingdom
Tel: +44 20 7766 7304
http://www.royalcollection.org.uk/visit/windsorca stle

Stonehenge
Address: Amesbury, Wiltshire SP4 7DE, United Kingdom
Tel: +44 870 333 1181
http://www.stonehenge.co.uk

Highclere Castle
Address: Highclere Park, Newbury, West Berkshire RG20 9RN, United Kingdom
Tel: +44 1635 253 210
http://www.highclerecastle.co.uk

To book a day trip:
http://www.londontoolkit.com/tours/premium_downton_abbey.htm

Meraz Café
Address: 56 Hanbury Street, London E1 5JL, United Kingdom
Tel: +44 20 7247 6999
http://merazcafe.co.uk

• Day 5 •

Today we'll offer a variety of options so you can enjoy a bit of unstructured time in London. So after a good breakfast, you can head wherever the wind blows you!

For sure, though, a must see in London is the **London Eye,** a gigantic Ferris wheel on the South Bank of the River Thames. Also called the Millennium Wheel, the "eye" has 32 passenger capsules, each representing one of the London boroughs. What stunning views of the city from inside! **It's loads of fun** and an awesome way to wrap up your time in London!

 You can also visit **Westminster Abbey** today! One of the city's major tourist attractions, Westminster Abbey features many amazing artifacts, including paintings, sculptures, stained glass, and textiles. Remember to wear appropriate clothing when visiting the church!

And how about a stroll or **guided tour** along the **River Thames**? The Thames is one of the most iconic landmarks of London and the views are fabulous — you can snap a few more shots of the city along the way. And be sure not to miss the famous canals as well, like Little Venice Canal and Regent's Canal.

And if you have time, definitely visit the West End's **Oxford Street** (packed with over 300 stores, so you might need an entire day to peruse here!), or the famous upmarket department store in Knightsbridge, **Harrods**, for some great shopping.

And perhaps a return to the enchanting **Covent Garden** for another round of **delicious fish and chips**? And then there's always a jaunt to Notting Hill's **Portobello Road** marketplace for great bargain and antiques shopping.

You'll undoubtedly come across great food options today as you go about, so we encourage you to try a couple for lunch and dinner today — enjoy!

Location Information

The London Eye
Address: London SE1 7PB, United Kingdom
Tel: +44 871 781 3000
https://www.londoneye.com

The Westminster Abbey
Address: 20 Deans Yd, London SW1P 3PA, United Kingdom
Tel: +44 20 7222 5152
http://www.westminster-abbey.org

Harrods
Address: 87-135 Brompton Road, London SW1X 7XL, United Kingdom
Tel: +44 20 7730 1234
http://www.harrods.com

Oxford Street (West End)
http://oxfordstreet.co.uk

Covent Garden (West End)
http://www.coventgardenlondonuk.com

Rock & Sole Plaice (Covent Garden)
Address: 9aj, 47 Endell Street, London WC2H 9AJ, United Kingdom
Tel: +44 20 7836 3785
http://www.rockandsoleplaice.com

Portobello Road Market (Notting Hill)
http://www.portobelloroad.co.uk

• Best Places For Travelers on a Budget •

Bargain London Sleeps

Stylotel London is a nice inexpensive option for accommodations in London. It is well located near Paddington Station and occupies a former townhouse. The rooms have a very ultra modern and futuristic look — and we think you'll find the lobby very interesting!

Stylotel London
Address: 160-162 Sussex Gardens, London W2 1UD, United Kingdom
Tel: +44 20 7723 1026
https://www.stylotel.com

Jesmond Hotel is located in Bloomsbury and is a really good value. It is a full English bed and breakfast close to the tube station as well as Oxford Street shopping. The rooms are small, but you can't beat the price.

Jesmond Hotel
Address: 63 Gower St, Bloomsbury, Gower Street, Fitzrovia, London WC1E 6HJ
Tel: +44 20 7636 3199
https://www.jesmondhotel.org.uk

Another good boutique hotel in Central London (in the trendy district of Kensington) is **Twenty Nevern**

Square. This hotel is in a Victorian townhouse that has about 20 individually designed rooms. We think it's definitely a prime location with reasonable nightly rates.

Twenty Nevern Square
Address: 20 Nevern Square, London SW5 9PD, United Kingdom
Tel: +44 20 7565 9555
http://www.20nevernsquare.com

Bargain London Eats

The Stockpot is a well-established comfort food London restaurant. The budget-friendly and filling food is particularly great on cold and rainy days!

The Stockpot
Address: 18 Old Compton Street, London W1D 4TN, United Kingdom
Tel: +44 20 7287 1066
http://www.stockpotlondon.co.uk

For delicious natural, ethnic food, check out **Koshari Street** restaurant. They offer inexpensive vegetarian, Egyptian fare with a modern twist. The décor is cool, with modern looking wall cartoons. You can dine inside or takeaway.

Koshari Street
Address: 56 Saint Martin's Lane, London WC2N 4EA, United Kingdom
Tel: +44 20 7836 1056
http://www.kosharistreet.com

And of course a trip to London would not be complete without a bite or two of delicious Indian food. Check out **Meraz Cafe**. It's on a side road in the Brick Lane area, away from the crowds. And definitely order the delicious curry chicken or any of their other yummy dishes.

Meraz Cafe
Address: 56 Hanbury Street, London E1 5JL, United Kingdom
Tel: +44 20 7247 6999
http://merazcafe.co.uk

• Best Places For Ultimate Luxury •

Luxury London Sleeps

For the best luxury experience, we're sending you to the **Mandarin Oriental** in London's famed Hyde Park. They offer world-class lavish services, incredible amenities and spa treatments—not to mention the splendid views of Hyde Park!

Mandarin Oriental
Address: 66 Knightsbridge, London SW1X 7LA, United Kingdom
Tel: +44 20 7235 2000
http://www.mandarinoriental.com/london

Another high-class luxury experience is at **Claridge's** in Mayfair. Now here's a renowned hideaway for kings, queens, and the have mores. The elevator harkens back to a bygone era—you'll find a comfortable seat and uniformed attendant. Have your afternoon tea to melodic violin strains in the Grand Foyer—an atmospheric treat!

Claridge's
Address: Brook Street, Mayfair, London W1K 4HR, United Kingdom
Tel: +44 20 7629 8860
http://www.claridges.co.uk

And our final luxury recommendation is **The Goring** hotel, located just a 10-minute walk from Buckingham Palace. This historic hotel remembers the old days of the city well. It features a large private garden with some of the most beautiful flowers and plants. Well kept and well tended, each guest room is decorated with Gainsborough silk on the walls.

The Goring
Address: Beeston Place, London SW1W 0JW, United Kingdom
Tel: +44 20 7396 9000
http://www.thegoring.com

Luxury London Eats

Our recommendations are all **ultra-exclusive, well-patronized** locales. **Always call ahead for reservations** to ensure you'll have a table!

For a truly amazing dining experience don't miss **Sketch** in Mayfair. Sketch is one of London's most frequented and most expensive restaurants. They offer a high-end French menu, delicious desserts, cocktails and impressive wine options.

Sketch in Mayfair
Address: 9 Conduit Street, London W1S 2XG, United Kingdom
Tel: +44 20 7659 4500
http://sketch.london

Another upscale spot we've mentioned previously is **Maze Grill**, one of Gordon Ramsay's many restaurants. They also serve classic French cuisine. The food is absolutely amazing here and you'll love the chic, art deco décor!

Maze Grill
Address: 68 Royal Hospital Road, London SW3 4HP, United Kingdom
Tel: +44 20 7352 4441
https://www.gordonramsayrestaurants.com/maze-grill-royal-hospital-road

Lastly, we also recommend the **Marcus** restaurant in Wilton Place (Formerly Marcus Wareing at the Berkeley). It's a high-end modern English restaurant with international influences. The food is remarkable, full of flavor, and the décor is contemporary and ultra chic.

Marcus
Address: The Berkeley, Wilton Place, Knightsbridge, London SW1X 7RL, United Kingdom
Tel: +44 20 7235 1200
http://www.marcus-wareing.com

• London Nightlife •

Great Bars in London

Of course, London is a city very well known for having great bars and pubs. One of our favorites is **Ape & Bird**. This bar is a great secret in a typical, touristy area. It's where the locals and people in the know go for drinks!

Ape & Bird
Address: 142 Shaftesbury Avenue, Soho, London WC2H 8HJ, United Kingdom
Tel: +44 20 7836 3119
http://apeandbird.com

The Coach & Horses is another really good, unpretentious, old school spot in London, known for the great vegetarian cuisine. On Wednesdays and Saturdays, you'll find fun piano sing-alongs!

The Coach & Horses
Address: 26-28 Ray Street, Clerkenwell, London EC1R 3DJ, United Kingdom
Tel: +44 20 7278 8990
http://www.thecoachandhorsessoho.co.uk

Great Clubs in London

The Ministry of Sound is our first recommendation worth checking out. It's a cool flagship club in London's South Bank neighborhood.

Ministry of Sound
Address: 103 Gaunt Street, London SE1 6DP, United Kingdom
Tel: +44 870 060 0010
http://www.ministryofsound.com/club

Another hopping club on London's night scene is **Fabric** in Farringdon. It's a large club that gets very crowded if that's your thing. They play techno, house, dubstep and trance music tracks. Something for everyone!

Fabric
Address: 77A Charterhouse Street, London EC1M 6HJ, United Kingdom
Tel: +44 20 7336 8898
http://www.fabriclondon.com

Great Live Music in London

100 Club is one of the best live music spots in London. Once a basement jazz club, this Oxford Street venue is now a happening spot for a nice variety of live music entertainment.

100 Club
Address: 100 Oxford Street, London W1D 1LL, United Kingdom
Tel: +44 20 7636 0933
http://www.the100club.co.uk

For those who prefer a more cozy and intimate experience, **Windmill Brixton** is your spot! This venue also has a well-deserved reputation for championing new acts.

Windmill Brixton
Address: 22 Blenheim Gardens, London SW2 5BZ, United Kingdom
Tel: +44 20 8671 0700
http://windmillbrixton.co.uk

Great Theatre in London

You'll find the majority of London's theatres near Shaftesbury Avenue, the Strand, and neighboring streets in the West End. Be sure to check websites for show times and book your tickets well in advance for a great night at the theatre!

First, we highly recommend the **Shakespeare Globe Theatre.** This replica of Shakespeare's 16th century theatre was reconstructed about 200 yards from the original location.

Shakespeare Globe Theatre
Address: 21 New Globe Walk, Bankside, London SE1 9DT, United Kingdom
Tel: +44 020 7902 1400
http://www.shakespearesglobe.com

The Royal Court Theatre is considered 'the most important theatre in Europe' for its dedication to debuting performances and discovering new voices on the stage. It makes for a wonderful night at the theater!

Royal Court Theatre
Address: Sloane Square, Belgravia, London SW1W 8AS
Tel: +44 20 7565 5050
http://www.royalcourttheatre.com

The London Coliseum is a wonderfully historic building and an excellent place to enjoying remarkable opera, as well as great performances from the English National Ballet.

London Coliseum
Address: St Martin's Lane, Covent Garden, London WC2N 4ES
Tel: +44 20 7836 0111
http://www.eno.org

• Conclusion •

We 're sure you'll be impressed with the many dizzying attractions in and around this amazing city. From the London Eye that offers stunning views of the city, to the impressive range of museums and theaters in the West End, to the amazing shops, pubs, palaces and sporting venues (don't miss **Wembley Stadium**!), there's definitely something in London for everyone to enjoy. http://www.wembleystadium.com

So we hope you have found our guide to the historically cultured city of London helpful and wish you a safe, interesting, and fun-filled trip to England!

Warmest regards,

The Passport to European Travel Guides Team

Visit our Blog! Grab more of our signature guides for all your travel needs!

http://www.passporttoeuropeantravelguides.blogspot.com

★ **Join our mailing list** ★ to follow our Travel Guide Series. You'll be automatically entered for a chance to win a **$100 Visa Gift Card** in our monthly drawings! Be sure to respond to the confirmation e-mail to complete the subscription.

About the Authors

Passport to European Travel Guides is an eclectic team of international jet setters who know exactly what travelers and tourists want in a cut-to-the-chase, comprehensive travel guide that suits a wide range of budgets.

Our growing collection of distinguished European travel guides are guaranteed to give first-hand insight to each locale, complete with day-to-day, guided itineraries you won't want to miss!

We want our brand to be your official Passport to European Travel — one you can always count on!

Bon Voyage!

The Passport to European Travel Guides Team

http://www.passporttoeuropeantravelguides.blogspot.com

Made in the USA
Monee, IL
13 May 2020